Vertical Gardening 101

How to Create Your Vertical Urban Garden & Grow Healthy Organic Fruits & Vegetables

All Rights Reserved. No part of this publication may be reproduced in any form or by any means, including scanning, photocopying, or otherwise without prior written permission of the copyright holder. Copyright © 2014

Table of Contents

Introduction

Benefits of Vertical Gardening

Health Benefits

What is Vertical Gardening

History of Vertical Gardening

Father of Vertical Gardening

Media Types

Indoor Vertical Garden

Enclosed Vertical Garden

Cold Weather

Pest & Diseases

Tips for Vertical Gardening

Setting Up Your Vertical Garden

Compatible Foods & Flowers

Composting

Awareness is Key

Creative Recommendations

The Business of Vertical Gardening

Conclusion

Introduction

Thank you for downloading this book.

When it comes to creating your own garden, there are so many things that you have to consider. It isn't something you can plan overnight. It takes research and knowledge to find out exactly what is compatible with your lifestyle, the climate, and the soil you have outside.

Many people that want to try their hand at gardening always assumes that a garden means acres of land are needed. Somewhere flat, where the soil is rich in nutrients with a mild climate is most ideal. However, the new trend is to grow your garden vertically.

As more and more people are interested in gardening but do not want to give up living in the city for a hobby; vertical gardening was born. It is a great invention as space is valuable in the city and is never allotted for a full sized farm or vegetable patch. A vertical garden ensures that you can grow your own fruits and vegetables, get the best of the crop, and all be pesticide and chemical free!

There are many reasons why people elect to have a vertical garden. Apart from the obvious of accessibility and not having to give up the perks of city life to live on a farm, there are many other reasons. The vertical garden could finish off the design of your home, you are trying to lower your carbon footprint, or even because you want to take up a hobby to help relieve your stressful life, a vertical garden has many benefits.

Another great thing about vertical gardens are that they require significantly less time in comparison to a normal horizontal garden. The extra time will give you more time to enjoy the products of your crops versus tending to them.

Benefits of Vertical Gardening

There are many different benefits for the environment and your surroundings that come with vertical gardening. Some of them are listed below:

- Be able to have a garden despite the small space you have at home
- Grow different fruits and vegetables without worrying if they will starve off the other crops in your garden
- The vertical garden will shield the exterior of your house from harsh weather conditions
- Create an art piece
- Reduce your carbon foot print
- Save on electricity bills as the plants will act as a form of insulation and keep your house warmer in the winter and cooler in the summer
- Save on grocery bills
- Less weeds to remove
- Be able to have less amount of each plant without it looking sparse
- Increase animal habitats
- Grow a fence of fruits and vegetables that can also act as a privacy screen

- Have healthier plants (circulation of air improves as the plants are placed higher)
- Shade an area of the house that you want to keep darker
- Act as a divider for your yard or section rooms off using a vertical garden
- Conceal items such as the garbage and compost bin

Health Benefits

There are many health benefits for people that chose to build a vertical garden. Although there are some obvious benefits, there are also some surprising benefits that may increase your motivation to start a garden.

- It improves arthritis as you are doing a physical activity that requires you to be limber and flexible
- The plants in an urban living space increase motivation and focus to work on projects around the house.
- Having plants in or around the home promote a positive energy that reduces depression and anxiety
- Studies have shown having even a small vertical garden in an office increases the productivity of workers significantly.
- The plants breathe and absorb carbon monoxide, therefore improving the air quality
- Being able to stand and tend to your crops will mean there is less chance for strains and other muscle or soft tissue injuries.
- Have organic, pesticide, and chemical free produce that you know where it originates from.

- Plants will act as a dampener for noise and reduce the amount of disturbances from outside, therefore allowing you a haven to relax and reduce stress.

What is Vertical Gardening?

Vertical gardening is a technique that uses different resources to help the plants grow and extend upwards versus horizontally. It minimizes the need for support beams as plants generally want to grow upwards. The current trend is to use vertical gardening to remove the dull industrial design of the city and make the landscape more beautiful and versatile.

Vertical gardens are more popular as many people develop back pains when tending their garden. A vertical garden eliminates the need to bend over for long periods of time. It also saves a lot of space and a lot of time as a vertical garden contains much less digging around in the dirt.

Because there is less soil, weed is no longer a problem. Neither are animals such as bunnies, foxes, and dogs. Vertical gardens are usually made of planting pots instead of the soil in the ground. Seeds are placed into pots and built into the wall of the vertical garden. This will diversify your crop as you can grow as much or as little of a particular item as you wish. Many people have been using their creative side to create a live mural; using the colors of the flowers, they create a picture or pattern.

History of Vertical Gardens

A vertical wall is not something that is new. It is so ingrained in our daily lives that we often do not realize when there is a vertical garden present.

Vertical gardens can be both indoors and outdoors. They have been around since the Babylonian times. Back then, they mostly experimented with grapevines and ivy on trellises and walls. It wasn't until the 1920's that vertical gardens were bought into mainstream society. The British and Americans teamed up to promote and encourage adding gardens and plants to ones home.

From the late 1980's to early 1990's, vertical gardening was taken to a whole different level. Vertical gardens were finding popularity with major businesses such as airports as a unique feature could increase the popularity of the business. It was also during that time that businesses were more environmentally aware and wanted to reduce their carbon footprint.

It was not until the 21st century where vertical gardening has really taken off. Many cities are erecting large pieces of art that feature living murals and vertical gardens. More and more people living in urban cities are taking an interest as they want to know where their food comes from and is chemical free.

Father of Vertical Gardening

Patrick Blanc is often considered the father of modern day vertical gardening. He is a world renowned botanist that specializes in working with plants originating from the tropical forest.

Throughout his lifetime, he has created many works of art and won many awards for his concepts and creations. Blanc may not be the person that invented vertical gardening, but he is credited for modernizing and popularizing the concept of vertical gardening. Many consider Blanc as a scientist and an ecological engineer and he has won awards and recognition for his work in this field.

Patrick Blanc has been hired around the world to create living masterpieces. Some of his famous works can be seen in places such as the French embassy in New Delhi, 21st Century Museum of Contemporary Art in Japan, Melbourne Central Shopping Center in Australia, and The Athenaeum Hotel in London.

Media Types

Prior to creating a vertical garden, it is important to know which type of vertical garden is best suited for your home. There are three main media types that define a vertical garden. They are loose media, mat media, and structural media.

Loose Media

Loose media systems use soil in bag systems. Soil is placed into a bag and onto the wall. These vertical garden types require a full replacement of all supplies and systems at least once every year. The structure of the wall also needs to be replaced every two years. Loose Media vertical gardens are not suited for places that have a high chance of seismic activity as this garden has very loose soil and is more fragile. If damage occurs to the garden, repairs can only be done by replacing the entire bag or adding extra soil into any holes that may have appeared in the wall.

Loose media vertical gardens are not designed to be touched and interacted with by many people. These are gardens that need to be placed in private settings. These gardens are not suitable to be built over 8 feet high as they run the risk of being damaged by wind and rain.

Gardens with loose media are most suitable for gardeners who wish to change the plants from season to season or year to year.

Mat Media

Mat media vertical gardens are usually built with felt mats. As the felt mats are more thin, even if there were multiple layers of felt placed together, plants will need to be replaced every three to five years. This is because the roots of the plants start to become too intricate and heavy for the vertical garden to support it. Eventually, the roots will choke up the water system and nutrients of the other plants.

Repairing these systems require upgrading and changing the mats a section at a time. Often times, doing this results in damage to the neighboring plants and it is not recommended. The best is to replace the plants well before the five year mark.

Mat media vertical gardens grow best inside a building and are recommended for places that are earthquake proof. Small plants are recommended for this garden as larger plants may be too heavy and potentially rip through the mat and damage the plant below.

These vertical gardens are better as small systems as they do not hold water very well. They require an irrigation system and a buffer from the plant roots.

Structural Media

Structural media vertical gardens are great because they take the best of both the mat and loose media types, create a block and can be manufactured into different sizes.

These vertical gardens are great as the blocks do not degenerate and plants can be kept in the same pot for up to fifteen years. Many other aspects such as pH and water capacity can be customized in accordance to your garden.

These gardens are suitable for areas that have strong winds and have seismic activity. There are no height restrictions as these vertical gardens are generally quite resilient. These gardens tend to be more expensive to install, however the maintenance and repair costs are very low.

Indoor Vertical Garden

Indoor gardens are as easy as outdoor gardens. By choosing a wall inside of your home, you are able to plant more tropical weathered plants.

Despite it being warmer inside, the plants will still need sunlight to grow. If the plants cannot be placed near a window, then a sun lamp will be needed. However, there are plants that thrive best in the shade which may be more suitable for indoor life.

Ensure there is amply circulation in your home as the plants will need fresh air to grow.

Some plants that are suitable for indoor living conditions are the lipstick plant, sword ferns, rabbit's foot fern, wedding vines, and peace lilies.

Enclosed Vertical Gardens

Enclosed vertical gardens are similar to a green house building. The enclosed vertical garden will have a structure around it with the temperature set warmer than outside. However, there may not be enough sunlight which will compromise your plants. Either leave the top off of the structure or design a roof where sunlight, air, and rain can filter in.

As it is an enclosed vertical garden, there will be a need for a watering system. The plants will not survive on rain water alone. Heat sensitive plants are also not recommended to be placed within the enclosed garden.

Cold Weather

Although a vertical garden has many benefits, it is still a garden. This means that depending on the season, different plants can be grown. Consider that there are harvesting seasons and expect that there will be dormant time.

Outdoor vertical gardens are best started in the spring. It is the best time to plant your seed as there is ample rain and the temperature is no longer freezing.

Unless you are living somewhere that is warm all year round, there is not much you can do during the winter months. Instead, prepare the pots and soil for the spring time. Ensure you are keeping the soil rich and full of nutrients.

Also take this time to renovate and stabilize the structure of the vertical garden. The structure needs to be able to withstand strong gusts of wind and the weight of the pots and plants in the spring time.

Pests and Diseases

Although the garden is now vertical, it does not eliminate the risk of pests and diseases. Using homemade fertilizers will enable you to be conscious about any chemical reactions that the plants may have to the soil. Another way to prevent diseases is to rotate your crops. Rotating them will prevent soil borne diseases that may build due to have the same crop with the same soil year after year.

An organic way to get rid of pests is using a can of cola. Either have a glass of open cola close to the vertical garden or pour some directly into an empty pot on the wall. The sugar will attract the pests and they will drown or focus on the sugar. If there are already pests on your plants, it will sense the sugar and leave your plants to investigate.

Another way is to add flowers to your vertical garden. As many birds and larger insects feed on nectar, it will attract these species to your wall. With these species there, they will also rid you of small bugs or pests that may be detrimental to your plants.

Healthy plants are going to be the plants that have the best immune system. So a chemical free way to keeping your plants alive is to ensure they have a nutrient rich diet. A strong immune system will enable them to fight off any contagious disease that may crop up.

Consider adding natural plants and flowers that are natural bug repellents. Having a Venus Fly trap or another plant that repels bugs will minimize the chances of your other crops being damaged.

Weeds are less of a concern as there is less soil. It is very rare that the weeds will grow inside the pot itself. There may be some that grow between pots that need weeding, but the work will be much less compared to a horizontal garden.

Pesticides are almost always the last resort. The harsh chemicals inside pesticides prevent the plants from growing properly. It may also change the ecological balance of your garden and the destructive chemicals may kill off your plants. Also, pesticides are not something that should be ingested, therefore, using pesticides on your garden will mean the fruits and vegetables picked from the garden will contain pesticides. These pesticides will then make their way into your digestive system and could cause havoc.

Tips for Vertical Gardening

These are tips and things that need consideration prior to building your vertical garden.

- Use organic compost and fertilizers to prevent ingesting chemicals
- Consider whether the structure where the vertical garden is being built on permanent.
- Ensure the area that it is being built gets ample sunlight
- Consider how fast each plant grows. If the plants on top grow faster than ones placed on the bottom, it will cover up and shade the bottom plants.
- Ensure that the frame or structure can withstand the amount of weight that will be hanging from it
- The higher the plant is off the ground, the more it needs to be watered. They are exposed to more sun and wind, hence need more nutrients as well
- Ensure you have a plan for when a windy or stormy day. Make sure the structure is stable and secure.
- Less is more. Make sure there is enough room for each plant to grow comfortably.

Setting Up Your Vertical Garden

Research is first and foremost of the vertical garden. Plan and design how big and how you want the vertical garden to look. Spend some time in the nursery learning what grows best in the climate you live in.

The guidelines in this book are merely recommendations. Everything can be altered or changed to fit you and the needs of your garden.

1. Choose the right wall. The wall must be sturdy enough to hold some plants and their soil.
2. Purchase enough pots to fill your wall that are approximately 15 by 24 inches.
3. Fill each pot half full with soil
4. Place your seeds inside the pots.
5. Hang the pots in a row on the wall with metal grommets.
6. The order the pots should go is based on the seed type. Ones requiring more sunlight need to be at the top of the vertical garden.
7. Ensure each pot is at least six inches apart from the next.

Compatible Foods & Flowers

Vertical gardens are great and there are many fruit and vegetables that can be grown on the vertical garden. Most of these plants have an ability to thrive in most conditions. Below is a list of recommended plants that can get you started towards a healthier and greener lifestyle!

Tomatoes are able to grow up big and tall, which make them ideal to be planted in a garden that vertical. They are also easy to care for and are resilient.

Peas do not need to have a trellis to hold them up only grow to about six inches. However, they hold a large crop yield and grows very quickly. It is also a plant that can survive in more dynamic conditions.

Melons are a fruit that can grow on the wall. There are melons that are small enough to fit inside the planter and can hang comfortably from the wall.

Cucumbers are compatible with vertical gardens as they have vines that like to reach up. The actual plant itself will grow up to six inches only. These are light and durable

Pole beans have a similar structure as cucumbers, making it a great plant for your vertical garden. They like to climb upwards and can be a bit delicate.

Lipstick Plants are vibrant in color. They are also suitable for vertical gardens as they are resilient plants. They are able to thrive despite in drier conditions and poor lighting.

Sword Ferns are very easy to take care of. They are generally very healthy plants and are self sustaining. The only consideration is that it needs more water.

Wax Flowers are colorful and work as a pretty addition to your wall. It is suitable for a vertical garden as it is very flexible and will follow the direction you want it to grow.

Wedding Vines offer an amazing smell to your garden. It gives off a stronger fragrance than other plants, making it hugely popular. The best is that this plant will thrive in almost any condition.

Peace Lilies are no hassle plants. They require minimal care and are extremely easy to maintain. They will thrive in poor conditions with little light and little water.

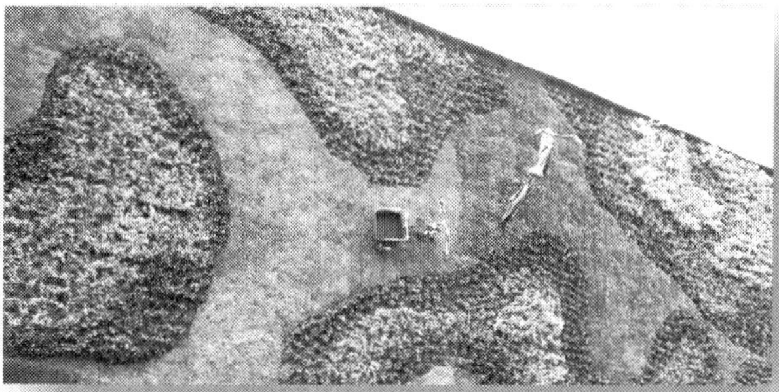

Composting

Using compost encourages the garden to grow. With a long term use of compost, the garden becomes stronger and more resilient, and is able to survive more sudden changes.

Composting can be made from lots of different ingredients. It is recommended that you store a large batch of compost in a garbage can so that you have enough for a month. A basic idea of what compost should include is:

- Pet feces
- Food scraps
- Wood chips
- Straw
- Grass clippings
- Vegetable stumps
- Fruit cores

Try not to open the composting bin too often as the items inside need to break down. It needs to sit at least one or two days untouched before it can be used. Being disturbed too much can cause the items to break down too much and lose some of the nutrients. Once it is ready to use, sprinkle it onto your crops for a better yield.

Awareness Is Key

Vertical gardens have many benefits. However, there are things that requires a little more attention.

- Vertical gardens tend to dry out faster than a horizontal garden. The sunlight will evaporate the water quickly. This means that the soil tends to lose its nutrients and the plants will be unable to continue growing.
- Space is limited in a vertical garden. It is difficult to grow larger plants as there is not enough space for the roots to expand past the pot. This limits what you can actually grow in your garden.
- Dirt tends to fall out of the pots as the wind and movement of the plants loosen the soil.
- Water can also pool at the bottom of the vertical garden or plug gutters and potentially damage the structure.
- The design and creation of the concept of a vertical garden is much more expensive. More equipment is needed for a vertical garden in comparison to a horizontal garden.

- A lot more planning has to go into the vertical garden before actually creating the garden.

Creative Recommendations

Vertical gardens are no longer just about gardening. Many urban farmers also care about how their garden looks. Whether it is matching the rest of the house or creating a live mural, these creative ideas we have included in the book should get your imagination going.

- Place a water fountain in the middle of your vertical garden will add a feeling of peace and tranquility
- Create a live mural of words instead of a picture or create a tribute to someone or something.
- Instead of using pots, use soda bottles. This is a great way to reduce the amount of plastic in the landfills.
- Add plastic totes on the side of your garden. These totes can be used to grow larger plants that may be too heavy for the actual garden.
- Gutters are a place to grow a micro-garden. It is creative, unique and makes use of a space that would have been otherwise left empty.
- Make your own felt pockets to grow the plants. The felt pockets can be colorful and felt is proven to be

able to hold enough water and soil for the plants to grow.

- Instead of a built wall, use different containers such as old cut out mail boxes, spice racks, and window boxes to build the vertical garden. It will add a unique touch and have a rustic feeling.

- Choose different size and color clay pots to build the garden. It will make certain areas of the garden or certain plants stand out. This way you can control what the viewers first see on the wall.

- Repurpose an old book shelf as the starting base of your vertical wall. They are durable and provide more and enough spacing for your plants to grow. Best of all, no measure is required to ensure the plants have enough room!

- Add a trellis for a Victorian feel. Not only will it look nice, it will help some of the plants that want to climb higher. Having vines climb around it will add a beautiful touch to your garden.

The Business of Vertical Gardening

More and more companies are starting up that offer vertical gardening services. For a fee, the company will design the garden based on your requests and come set it up for you. It is easy and convenient for someone that wants to tend to a garden but does not have the time to do the research and start up.

Most companies will come by your home to determine where the best place for the vertical garden to be built is. They will consider the lighting and air flow of the area and whether the plants you want to grow will be able to thrive there.

There is a need for these companies as many businesses want to promote that they are environmentally friendly. Having a vertical garden acts as a bold statement that demonstrates to customers where their priorities lie. It is also a way to reduce the carbon footprint that their business has on the environment.

Conclusion

Now that you know a little more about vertical gardens, we hope you will be influenced to create one. Although there are things to be aware of when building a vertical garden, the physical benefits and mental benefits far outweigh the concerns.

The vertical garden helps save lots of money in terms of food and electricity, but also helps protect your house from harsh weather conditions and the heat. Ailments such as arthritis and anxiety can be greatly reduced with a vertical garden.

By building a vertical garden, you are also giving back to the environment. By reducing the carbon footprint and making the urban areas more green, it will greatly improve your air quality and health.

Vertical gardens are great as they do not require you to give up your current lifestyle and can take the garden on as a hobby. It allows you to reap the benefits of knowing where your produce comes and healthier eating while not needing to give up the ease of city life.

Thank you for purchasing this book and we hope that you have gained some insight into vertical gardening.

Made in the USA
San Bernardino, CA
12 November 2016